SENSE AND SENSUALITY

JESUS TALKS WITH OSCAR WILDE ON THE PURSUIT OF PLEASURE

RAVI ZACHARIAS

Multnomah® Publishers *Sisters, Oregon*

SENSE AND SENSUALITY:
JESUS TALKS WITH OSCAR WILDE ON THE PURSUIT OF PLEASURE
published by Multnomah Publishers, Inc.

published in association with the literary agency of
Wolgemuth & Associates, Inc., 8600 Crestgate Circle, Orlando, Florida 32819

© 2002 by Ravi Zacharias
International Standard Book Number: 1-59052-014-9

Cover design by The Office of Bill Chiaravalle
Cover image by Photodisc

Unless otherwise indicated, Scripture quotations are from:
The Holy Bible, New International Version © 1978, 1984
by International Bible Society, used by permission of Zondervan
Other Scripture quotations:
The Holy Bible, New King James Version (NKJV) © 1984 by Thomas Nelson, Inc.

Multnomah is a trademark of Multnomah Publishers, Inc.,
and is registered in the U.S. Patent and Trademark Office.
The colophon is a trademark of Multnomah Publishers, Inc.

Printed in the United States of America

For information:
MULTNOMAH PUBLISHERS, INC. • P.O. 1720 • SISTERS, OREGON 97759

Library of Congress Cataloging-in-Publication Data
Zacharias, Ravi K.

Sense and sensuality: Jesus talks with Oscar Wilde on the pursit of pleasure / Ravi Zacharias.

p. cm.

ISBN 1-59052-014-9 (Hard Printed Case Side)

1. Wilde, Oscar, 1854–1900—Fiction. 2. Jesus Christ—Fiction. 3. Imaginary conversations.
4. Pleasure. I. Title.

PS3576.A19 S46 2002

813' .54—dc21

2002007491

02 03 04 05 06 07 08 — 10 9 8 7 6 5 4 3 2 1 0

To the youth of this world—
that sense would prevail over sensuality.

ACKNOWLEDGMENTS

There are three people in particular to whom I am indebted for bringing this manuscript to print: Danielle DuRant—as always, brilliant in her research; my wife, Margie—ever meticulous in her editing; and Rod Morris—skillful in simplifying the text without losing any of the depth.

My thanks to them all.

INTRODUCTION

Few figures in literature merit both genuine admiration and profound pity as much as Oscar Wilde. He was a genius. Yet sadly, he floundered and struggled with habits and propensities that ultimately crushed him beneath their weight. As I read and re-read his biographies, at times my heart ached for him in his struggles, and at other times I marveled at the sheer folly with which he threw his life away. Like an object caught in the tension of two opposing forces, his body and mind were torn between the love of God and the enticement of the sensual.

Playwright, dramatist, poet, critic—he was all of these things. But perhaps more than anything else, in his style and his intoxicated autonomy, he symbolizes the spirit of our age (though he died about a century ago in November 1900) because he was obsessed with art and pleasure for their own sakes. Such preoccupation reveals not only a pursuit, but also a struggle—that of finding a home for the imagination and the emotions. In such a pursuit there is a subtle jettisoning of absolutes. The aesthete is "Lord of the universe" and needs no other justification. Wilde castigated anyone who tried to take away his right to live with sensual abandon and enjoyment. He took charge of any conversation in any gathering and would draw the attention of everyone whenever he walked into a room. His attire was purposefully selected for each occasion, and arrayed in a riot of color, he would balloon into a room and take center stage. He truly could have sung the song "(I Did It) My Way."

Some people elicit a cultic following because they pursue such adulation. Others live with great arrogance and redefine everything in their wake. Their carefree iconoclasm attracts followers who idolize their free spirit. It was said of Wilde that he went to Oxford to pit himself against the most ancient university in England. The truth is that he was pitting himself against the most respected virtues throughout time.

At the same time, his was a dark and scary personality because the admixture of truth and error mangled his mind, and he suffered much from it. His death at forty-six was attributed to the destruction he brought upon his body through an indulgent lifestyle. Only recently have some discounted that his death was brought on by a syphilitic condition. That aside, the description of his death would grieve and possibly nauseate even his most hardened critic.

If there is one of his works that captures both his dream and nightmare life, it is *The Picture of Dorian Gray*. So profound is that book that it merits being described as one of the most true-to-life stories ever told. I have drawn from it in the dramatic narrative.

For these reasons, I selected Oscar Wilde as the conversationalist with Jesus. Pleasure was everything to him, but grief and pity followed his pleasure-mad ways. This is something that we need to understand in our times. But I have also introduced Blaise Pascal as a third member in this discussion. When I first selected Pascal, I did not know that one of the books Wilde read when he was imprisoned was Pascal's *Pensées*. My original reason for bringing Pascal into the conversation was that both Wilde and Pascal are buried in Paris and share a connection with the same church in Paris, Saint-Germain-des-Prés.

Pascal, as some may recall, is known as the father of the modern computer. A brilliant mathematician, he came to a conversion experience quite dramatically, such that he penned the story on a piece of paper and sewed it into the lining of his jacket. The one word that captured that conversion was *fire*. That description and that coat are kept in the archives of the Church of Saint-Germain-des-Prés. It was in the same church that Wilde's memorial service was held, some two centuries later. It is nestled in one of Paris's busy quarters and surrounded today by Parisian freedoms and, yes, various indulgences that Wilde would have loved and Pascal would have mourned. And it provides a backdrop to their two lives and to the differences in thinking between one who abandoned himself to the body and the other who was passionately devoted to matters of the soul. Pascal said, "It is in vain, oh men, that you seek within yourselves the cure for all your miseries." Wilde heard his mother say to a younger man, "When you are as old as I am, young man, you will find out that the only thing worth living for is sin." He embodied that pronouncement and, in his own words, found it to be bitter gall.

In this imaginary conversation, I hope you will carefully think through what is being said by each one. The words of Pascal and Wilde are not hard to imagine. They are borrowed either directly from what they said or clearly implied by their writings. In Jesus' case, I have used not only His words, but also words from other Scripture writers such as Solomon, who would have found some of Wilde's thinking similar to some of his own.

There may be no more important question in our time than the question of pleasure as it relates to life's purpose and meaning. You will have to judge whose words prove to be true in their reflection of reality.

One more thing: God is not against pleasure. His Word says that at His right hand are pleasures forevermore (see Psalm 16:11, NKJV). Let us begin this journey and see what He meant by that.

PROLOGUE

It was a cold and windy day in Paris, just two days after the unforgettable attack on the World Trade Center in New York and the Pentagon near Washington. My mind was already sobered by those events. I had begun my journey to track the life and thinking of Oscar Wilde. I had rented a car and driven to the historic Père Lachaise cemetery. The vast spread of land before me was quite daunting. I stopped at the gate and asked the guard to direct me to the grave of Oscar Wilde, and unhesitatingly he pointed the directions, as if he had been asked that question hundreds of times before. I drove to his grave, where I found a massive phoenix monument. On one side of it is a stanza from his powerful poem, *The Ballad of Reading Gaol:*

And alien tears will fill for him
    Pity's long-broken urn,
For his mourners will be outcast men,
    And outcasts always mourn.

I sat there a while, reading the rest of the poem until two young people came by, one of them blind and walking with the assistance of her friend. They spoke a language I did not understand. Cemeteries are lonely places, but one of the best places to think of life's short span.

The two young people asked if I could explain what was written on the other side of the tombstone. But alas, between their language and mine, I could not convey to them what the Scripture from the book of Job meant. That simple incident only reinforced the message of Oscar Wilde's life: It is very hard to be certain of what transpired within him as he came to the end of his days.

Moving on from the cemetery, I spent an hour at the Church of Saint-Germain-des-Prés, pondering the memorial service held there for him. The church was filled with visitors coming to pray following the terrorist attacks in the United States. Such horror drives people into churches. The images of grief and helplessness were written large on every face. It was no different in Wilde's life: In the end, it was the church that he turned to as sorrow gripped his own conscience.

Tragedy seems a strange sentiment to feel when considering the life of one so recklessly committed to drinking the cup of pleasure to the last drop—but ironically, it is the most appropriate feeling. Such a storm is created in one's heart by the clashing of emotions! How does one sift through the conflicting sentiments at the end of his life? I let my mind wander to that bed-side in his hotel room where he lay a hundred years ago—and the conversation begins.

SENSE AND SENSUALITY

JESUS TALKS WITH OSCAR WILDE ON THE PURSUIT OF PLEASURE

Oscar Wilde: *(Speaking to the nurse after another injection of morphine)* Another stab, another momentary respite from hell! You know, I thought living exacted all the pain there was to exact. I didn't know that dying possessed its own stock of torture. Would somebody write to my friend Robbie in London and tell him that I'm dying beyond my means? Tell him to hurry and come.

Robert Ross: I'm here, Oscar. I'm here. I was planning to come later this month, but when I heard how close to death you were, I took the boat over.

Wilde: Thank heavens; I'm so glad you're here. So it all ends in this dilapidated bohemian structure, l'Hôtel d'Alsace, 13 Rue des Beaux-Arts. Maybe they should put number thirteen on my hearse. Quite fitting…the final address for a homeless man. Just look at this place. It tells a story, doesn't it?

Ross: So here in France they call this a suite, eh? But considering you have nothing to pay, I would stomach this if I were you. Although this thick red-velvet curtain around your bed is somewhat like a shroud. I could help tidy up, I suppose, by cleaning up these cheap French-cigarette ashes littering your floor.

Wilde: Don't move any books or papers, Robbie. A room full of papers and books scattered all over is a tribute to a literary mind. And by the way, I like the red.

Ross: I'm glad you haven't completely lost your sarcastic tongue!

Wilde: I'll tell you what…I'm not sarcastic about that horrid wallpaper with its anemic-looking flowers. One of us has to go, Robbie, either the wallpaper or I.

Ross: Right now it looks like the wallpaper is winning. It's so dark and damp in here. Nothing we can do about it, I guess.

Wilde: Yes, the morgue yawns for me, Robbie. I'd like to take a walk one more time. But I seem to move in and out of reality. I was thinking…I have tricked my way out of everything; I might work on a plan to trick my way out of death, too. What do you think? Maybe when that trumpet sounds the last judgment, I shall just pretend that I have not heard it.

No, the laughter is dead, I'm afraid. This nausea, this constant spitting of blood. It's awful, Robbie. My throat is a limekiln, my brain a furnace, and my nerves a coil of angry adders.

Can you give me a glass of that absinthe there, please?

Ross: You're not supposed to drink that, Oscar. The doctors have ordered you to stay away from it.

Wilde: Since when have I taken orders from anybody? I simply can't believe they've got this right, that this death-breeding spore has made its way into my spine. Ah! Remorse is but a beggar's refuge.

Maybe when that trumpet
sounds the last judgment,
I shall just pretend that
I have not heard it.

OSCAR WILDE

Ross: What do you mean by "death-breeding spore"?

Wilde: One doctor has finally diagnosed what has brought on this meningitis, you know.

Ross: What is it?

Wilde: What I just said. This is an attack of tertiary syphilis, he says. This death knell hangs over me from that fateful night three decades ago.

Ross: Are you sure?

Wilde: That's what he tells me for now, but how can I be sure? Frankly, I don't think it has anything to do with syphilis. I think it has to do with this deadly pain in my middle ear. The ear surgery for that fall I took in prison has done nothing to help. But when you've lived the way I have, they can get you to believe anything about the aches of your anatomy.

Ross: No doubt.

Wilde: Sometimes I feel like I'm supping with the dead; at other times I feel the Christ I have battled all my life near at hand. Some things I see very clearly—that zinc box readied for me that goes beneath the earth as if to cover up what one really is. At other times my head is overcome by a wave of ghostly personalities seeking to drag me in different directions.

Ross: Should I talk to the nurse about giving you a larger dose of morphine?

Wilde: No. The morphine doesn't work anymore.

Ross: Then why not—

Wilde: Quiet! Please, Robbie! Silence! Don't disturb this vision. Here it comes again! Look at the size of this cemetery! The famed Père Lachaise, ground for the great. Hundreds of thousands lie beneath. You know, Napoleon opened this cemetery. A whole city of death! Some say about a million. What names, now food for worms—Balzac, Abelard, La Fontaine. None speaking now except...

Ross: You're slipping away, Oscar. You're not in a cemetery. You're—

Wilde: You know, Napoleon asked to be buried here, too. Maybe...maybe this spot is reserved for me. But I don't want it here. Bagneux is better, more genteel. You know, I often said that if a man needed a large tombstone in order to remain in the memory of his countrymen, then his living itself would've been an act of absolute superfluity.

I think I see the gardener... Tell me, sir, will it be a large tombstone?

Ross: Don't go! Oscar!

Wilde: Excuse me, Gardener! Don't walk so fast. Talk to me. Do you tend all these graves yourself?

Are you real, or am I just talking to the wind here? Who

are you? I'm not going to miss these Parisian winters anymore, that's for certain. But please say something.

Gardener: I wasn't able to get your attention most of your life, Oscar. Now all of a sudden you want me to talk to you?

Wilde: Why do I think you are…?

Gardener: Aren't you the very one who said that if I am perfect, I cannot relate to you? What do you want from me now?

Wilde: I should've known! I should've known! You've been mistaken for a gardener before, haven't you? Are you the Christ I'm talking to? You know, I've not done well with gardens and gardeners before.

Gardener: I know you haven't.

Wilde: You know it well, then. Life seems to start off that way: a garden before you…

Gardener: It did once upon a time.

Wilde: As I look back, my only mistake was that I confined myself so exclusively to the trees of what seemed to me the sunlit side of the garden and shunned the other side for its shadow and its gloom.

Gardener: Your pain is intense now. What do you want from me? To help you escape once more?

Wilde: Look what I'm reduced to: failure, disgrace, poverty, sorrow, despair, suffering, tears even, broken words that come from lips of pain, remorse that makes one walk on thorns, a conscience that condemns, self-abasement that punishes, misery that puts ashes on one's head, and anguish that chooses sack-cloth for its raiment and into its own drink puts gall. I often said that I wished I could look into the seeds of time to see what was coming.

Gardener: You've always had a way with words, dear Oscar! You've come to the right place to see what comes to everyone.

You did ask who I am, didn't you?

Wilde: I did. I'm somewhat fearful of the answer. Can I bring Robbie into this discussion? I'm unsure of myself when facing you alone. Can—

Gardener: Not right now. Believe me; he'll have his turn. His mind, he thinks, is very clear and yours is confused. But not long after you have gone, he's going to come looking for me, too. But this is a time for you and me to—

Wilde: My heart is pounding like a hammer within me. This can't be true. I can't get it to stop its blows.

I was fearful of meeting up with you, after all. All my life you've haunted me. I've sought to flee from you. You are…you are… Tell me. You are—

Gardener: Do you really want to know?

How could You be the perfect
soul and still feel what we
humans do at the same time?
That has to be the greatest
puzzle.

OSCAR WILDE

Wilde: Yes, I've played word games all my life. But time has squeezed me out of playing time. I was afraid of all these things and had determined to know nothing of them, yet I was forced to taste each of them in turn, to feed on them, to have for a season no other food at all. No, I have not escaped.

But here I go again. It's true. I'm afraid it's true. I've done well, talking all my life. I need to listen, don't I? I can't afford the luxury of toying with you. The Christ! You are, aren't you?

Jesus: I am, I am. I wanted to meet you now while there's still time for you. Just a few hours, to be sure. This day was written in the heart of My Father long before it came to be.

This isn't the best way to meet. Somehow over your lifetime you were delighted to live with a warring conscience. In fact, you still struggle.

Wilde: I was a master of duplicity and was always thinking I could win at the game.

Jesus: Trifling with truth? A costly game.

Do you remember what your friend said of you: "walking backwards toward the altar with your eye ever on the exit"? And on another occasion, the letter written to you after you went to church on one occasion, cautioning you not to toy with things sacred? Do you ever think of those things?

Wilde: How well I remember those words and that letter! Where do I begin? I just never thought You divine, Lord Christ.

How could You be the perfect soul and still feel what we humans do at the same time? That has to be the greatest puzzle to me.

Jesus: You have often called Me by My title. Let Me speak to you now, Oscar, you who once brimmed with confidence but are now only a shadow of yourself. What your imagination feared and your arguments resisted meet in this cemetery—only reversed. Now your arguments make you fearful and your imagination resists this common event happening every day for somebody in this world.

Wilde: I've longed to know what Your voice sounded like. The Scriptures speak of Your voice as the sound of rushing waters. Quite a metaphor! But here You are, strong and gentle at once. Please keep speaking. The words seem more like arrows of truth piercing the armor of my pretense. My mask is falling to pieces before me.

Jesus: This is where I begin to question you, since you've been so unabashed about your questioning of God.

Do you who argued all your life about the breadth of the imagination limit God's ability to combine His mind and the need of humanity in one person—Myself? Where was your own imagination when you thought that was impossible? And by the way, as for this "perfect soul" puzzle of yours...is it because you despise any form of reproof? Where were you, Oscar, when the imagination was framed in the mind of My Father? What do you know about the enduring nature of the soul that you flirted with it in your writings as just another means to play with words? And one more thing…"soulishness" belongs to humanity. I am life itself. It's not something I possess. It's what I am. You are the receptor. I am the giver.

Wilde: I feel like Job on the receiving end of the flurry of questions You rained on him.

Jesus: Keep thinking about Job. You'll be borrowing some words from him for your tombstone. My Word seems to provide expression for many people as they feel the need to speak, even from the grave.

Wilde: So, will it be a big tombstone? Not from my estate, I'm sure.

Jesus: That's not important now, is it?

Wilde: Can we take a walk somewhere else? Somehow, cemeteries scare me a bit, because I'm not quite sure that there's just nothing there. I once said that hell would be the body existing without the soul or the soul existing without the body. I'm terribly nervous that I'm on the verge of tearing asunder what You've joined together!

Jesus: I'd be pleased to walk with you anywhere, not just through this cemetery. But I want to take you through some familiar places to bring to mind the struggle of your soul. In each of these settings you reached out to Me, but with a divided heart.

Wilde: Struggle is a mild word; torture would be more appropriate.

Jesus: The eye of the needle was too narrow for you, though I offered to pull you through.

Wilde: True.

Jesus: You misjudged where freedom lay, Oscar.

Wilde: Then why are You leading me toward the side of town that brought me the weight of sorrow I now bear?

Jesus: I walk these streets every night because this is where life's biggest mistakes are made. And this is where the most wounded and hurting spirits walk in shells of bodies—the living dead. This is where they begin to forcibly separate what I have joined together. They're like men walking to their graves in the dark, blinded by these colored lights...to the sepulchres they are being dragged by the seducers of their imagination. They call these the streets of pleasure. How untrue! How deceitful! How destructive! I hear more screams from here at daybreak than I do from beds of sickness.

Wilde: I'm one of them! All that pleasure offered turned out to be a path to much loss, and all that I shunned about pain I found to be the path to ultimate gain. You know well how I roundly rejected laws! I insisted that I was made for exceptions. My mother and I were serious about forming a society that was against the practice of virtue.

Jesus: That state of mind cost you everything you really wanted, Oscar. You know, when you were in prison, you made it a point to read the Gospels and the Epistles every night. By the way, your insistence on reading them in Greek made the angels smile at the size of your ego, even in your state of humility. Even in your search beyond yourself, your self loomed large.

Wilde: Well, I'm a stickler for words, and I didn't want anyone hiding from me what was originally said. You know that one of my more famous lines was that we in England have a lot in common with America, except the language!

Jesus: Yes…or should I say, yeah?

Wilde: So You do have a sense of humor! I was so afraid that everything would be heavy in Your presence. But before I forget, we also have seldom read what lies beyond our own language and—

Jesus: Have missed the laws of truth that underlie life.

Wilde: Precisely. I guess it's possible to keep rules in areas of learning but forget rules in morality.

Jesus: It's been another one of the great struggles of the human heart. But you, too, would've brought yourself a great deal of personal benefit if you'd seen the Gospels in the light of the law as My Father revealed it through the prophets. Your aversion for laws was misguided. You should've understood their place in your happiness.

Wilde: That was no doubt my problem—laws, restrictions, rules, boundaries! Why such inhibition? An imprisonment of the will, even as the imagination roams free! That's the one thing about Christianity that causes convulsions in my thinking.

Jesus: The abuse of law is commonplace. I remember a woman being dragged before Me for her adultery—her accusers sought her life. You should've seen their masks fall off when, confronted by their own duplicity, one by one they began to walk away.

Wilde: To me, that was one of the most moving stories in the Gospels—that and the one of the woman who broke her alabaster flask to lavish fragrant perfume over You. My! How those pharisaical disciples sneered at her presence and the liberty she had taken with You!

Jesus: Yes, they're precious enough stories to be told wherever My gospel is preached. So let Me ask you this: Why did you vehemently resist laws that restricted your appetites yet convulse in anger that society didn't have rules to govern its treatment of prisoners?

Wilde: I'm not used to being checkmated like this! But it gets a bit more complex than my objections, I think. I agree that I spent myself in sexual indulgence. But I don't believe that my anger at the way society abused me is misplaced. In prison they tortured me through hunger, insomnia, and disease. I've been exposed naked, as it were, before a mocking world. Yes, I burn inside with an unquenchable hate toward them for what they've done to me!

Jesus: Prison reveals the limitations of the law, Oscar. If anything, prison should show to humanity the weakness of human power, not its strength. There are many who cry out to Me in prison, and I visit them. And there are many who visit those in prison in My name. In a strange way, a prison is a microcosm of life itself.

Wilde: I can see that.

Jesus: People find ways to break free, only to find that freedom isn't so much external as it is internal. When the law is written on one's heart, it brings freedom. Prison presents a person with the choice to change within and be free or be violent within and remain bound. That may be why so many people meet Me there, sensing their own powerlessness to change and longing for a higher law. Why, you yourself... But let Me ask you—

Wilde: Yes, I cried out to You. But the law, I mean the system—

Jesus: In all your anger against the system, did you really expect society to turn a blind eye to the youths whom you yourself admitted that you hurt? You demanded of society that it change the way it treats prisoners. If society has a responsibility toward those who've committed crimes against humanity, doesn't it have a greater responsibility to protect those against whom the crimes are committed?

Wilde: Please, do we have to go into all of that?

Jesus: I have spoken My strongest words against those who destroy young lives, lives in the fresh bloom of youth, trampled underfoot by the callousness of self-gratification.

Wilde: I writhe in pain over some of those mistakes.

Jesus: Laws are like fences that a community erects for the safety of all. Those who understand best the human capacity for evil understand the need for laws. Those who understand the human heart best see the limitation of laws. I know best the human heart's ability to twist laws till nobody understands their purpose anymore.

Wilde: And the day will come—believe me it will—when sexual choices cannot be legislated; then society will have reached its ideal state by not interfering with the proclivities of people!

Jesus: Just because society may change its laws governing sexual behavior doesn't mean the change will be for the better. If society

Laws are like fences

that a community erects

for the safety of all.

JESUS

were to change its laws to legitimize the victimization of a race, would you affirm that as good also? Do you remember reading the story of the woman I spoke to at the well? She would be blocked out of heaven if some had their way.

Wilde: Forgive me for remaining silent. You know…you know…when I was a mere thirteen years old, I won a prize for Scripture knowledge and memorization.

Jesus: And received Butler's *Analogy of Religion* as a reward.

Wilde: Talking about religion, I love this church, Saint-Germain-des-Prés. It's so peaceful in here…so close to the bustle of this city, yet so far from its noise and clamor.

Jesus: Much has transpired in here over the centuries.

Wilde: Oh, I know it well—the oldest belfry in Paris, a good nine hundred years old; nine chapels in there, I believe; the magnificent Romanesque architecture; its gold and purple grandeur; the echo of quiet voices. I've been here many times before. I spent many quiet hours here, pondering my soul. But my life is now like an echo with no music of its own.

Jesus: The next time you're spoken of here, you will not be here. But some of those who cherished you and your works will be gathered here for a memorial service.

Wilde: This is where it will be?

Jesus: You still care, do you? It's a strange feature about humans…to be concerned about fame even when they're not there to enjoy it.

Wilde: Death is a horrible thing, Lord Christ. So final, so consummate.

Jesus: I understand. I wept at the grave of a friend, too, and it's a mystifying thing for humans to see My eyes filled with tears, as if I'm removed from their pain. But I feel pain differently from anyone else ever, because I'm able to feel pain without being broken by sin. Just as I see death without finality.

This is what I want you to understand, Oscar. You see, tears can be shed from a different kind of pain. When you experience pain that comes from being broken by sin, you see only the past and the present. I see pain differently, because I experience it without sin. It's a pain so pure that it actually is a chosen sorrow in time, while seeing every tear through the lens of eternity. But we will get to that later.

Wilde: I wish we could talk about this more.

Jesus: I can assure you we will. Let's step inside. I think you might enjoy a quiet spot. And I want you to meet somebody. He understood law and its demands very well.

Wilde: Who is it? Somebody who works here?

Jesus: You'll find out.

Wilde: But won't You be recognized if You walk in?

When you experience pain that

comes from being broken by sin,

you see only the past

and the present.

I see pain differently,

because I experience it

without sin.

JESUS

Jesus: I'm afraid that sometimes a church is the last place I'm recognized.

Wilde: Like the episode of "The Grand Inquisitor," I guess.

Jesus: Exactly. Sometimes My presence is just too discomfiting to those wrapped up in "worship." Anyhow, I want you to meet this person. Actually, you've met him before, so I shall save the introductions. There he is, seated at that table. He's expecting us. This will take just a few moments, Oscar. I think you'll enjoy this.

Stranger: Monsieur Wilde, I presume?

Wilde: We've met? Pardon me for not remembering.

Jesus: Well, it's never been face-to-face. But he has some things to share with you that I think will stir your heart, as he's done before.

Wilde: I can't miss an authentic French accent when I hear one. So do we speak in French?

Stranger: No, let's keep it in English; otherwise I'm afraid that between the three of us, we might get into a lighthearted discussion about which language is the most heavenly. And He who is the Word will have the last word on that...unless you want to speak in Aramaic?

Wilde: No, English is fine. But who are you, anyway? You sound rather learned, and your face—

Stranger: Let's just say that my thinking has deeply affected you, and my thoughts have made an impact on your life, though we've never met.

Wilde: Even as a child I didn't enjoy such games. But here I am dying and having to play one!

Stranger: I believe you'll enjoy this one, though. Come to the back room in this church. You don't recognize my face, but you might recognize my coat.

Wilde: This is getting stranger by the minute. Tell me, Lord Christ, what—

Jesus: Leave Me out of this for the moment. I just arranged the meeting. I did this once for My disciple Peter. Do you remember the mountaintop experience where he met Moses and Elijah? I should say that he didn't want to leave the spot. You'll not want to either. But you have very limited time, Oscar, before you must leave this place. So listen well.

Wilde: But this is no mountain, no shining-white Transfiguration, no Moses and Elijah here. What's this tattered coat supposed to mean? It looks a good two hundred years old to me.

Stranger: You're right. Now look on the inside and see what's sewn there. No, no, don't rip it off! For a man who fancied clothing, you certainly show no respect for—

Wilde: If you don't mind my saying this, this coat wouldn't have made it into my wardrobe.

Stranger: No doubt. But how would you like me to rip apart one of your famed first editions?

Wilde: I'm sorry, but I can't see this being compared to my first editions.

Stranger: Do you see this paper sewn into the lining? Here's a copy of what's penned there.

Wilde: May I read it?

Stranger: Yes, but in English, please, and we shall test your translation skills.

Wilde: "Monday, 23 November, 1654. From about half past ten in the evening until about half past midnight—Fire. The God of Abraham, the God of Isaac, the God of Jacob. Not of the philosophers and intellectuals. Certitude, certitude. Jesus Christ...may I never be separated from Him."

Why on earth have you given me this to read? These are the words of Blaise Pascal. His famed conversion, his "night of fire." Are you...are you...?

Pascal: Delighted to meet you, Monsieur Wilde. Two hundred and forty-eight years later, to the day. I was a mathematician, you know, but who's counting anymore? And, by the grace of

Christ, here in the same church where a record of my memorial service is kept in the archives and yours is but a few days away.

Wilde: The famed author of *Pensées!* Lord Christ, what can I say? Monsieur Pascal, I'm so sorry about that comment about your coat and its lack of style.

Pascal: Quite fitting for a professorial mind, don't you think?

Wilde: I shall not incriminate myself any further. This is utterly incredible! I wish Robbie could see this. If there were any two persons before whom I'd bow my head, they would be you and the Lord Christ. Your thoughts and His presence carried me through my most bitter years.

Pascal: You don't need to bow before me. The one before whom we all bow makes the greatest dreams of our lives possible, and He is here. Without Him, life would be a nightmare.

Wilde: Yes, we were just talking about that. I think you and I came to two different conclusions early in life, and that made the difference in the way we lived.

Pascal: You looked for proof and despised limitations. I insisted that proof had its limitations, while the law of God was boundless.

Wilde: You sort of went against the disciplines, didn't you?

Pascal: Not quite. The most misunderstood aspect of my writings was the slanderous attempt by many to say that I was against reason. Not one whit of truth in that! I've always stressed the place of reason—inductive, direct, experimental, empirical, and so on. But every discipline must be governed by certain laws. You understand those laws, and you revel in the discipline. You ignore those laws, the discipline collapses. I wanted the mind to understand the heart as well.

Wilde: You don't waste any time getting to the point, do you?

Pascal: I have all the time in the world. It is you who—

Wilde: By the way, tell me…is it true that at the age of twelve you had figured out on your own the Euclidean formula that the sum of the angles of a triangle is equal to two right angles?

Pascal: Oh my! Here we go again. I had to answer that question so many times. Yes, it is true, M. Wilde. It turned out to be quite an emotional day in the household, to say the least.

Wilde: And you had a calculating machine to your credit by the time you were twenty-one?

Pascal: A cumbersome thing, it was. It took me two years to perfect it. It seems so comical now. But there was a time when it was fun. All of that's now past.

Wilde: Yes, but what a life you lived! Such genius wrapped up in such a brief window of time!

Pascal: But what is this you're saying about *my* being a genius? I've heard—

You looked for proof
and despised limitations.
I insisted that proof
had its limitations,
while the law of
God was boundless.

BLAISE PASCAL

Wilde: Well, yes, I have to say it's true. Even in school I could read a three-volume set of books with terrifying speed before a day was over and remember its content well.

Jesus: You're both beginning to sound like a couple of brothers I know whose mother tried to make a reservation for them in heaven!

Pascal: Sorry, Lord. Yes, that was somewhat humorous. Everyone is ignorant, M. Wilde, only in different subjects.

Wilde: My apologies, too. Pride is one thing that possibly separated you from me, M. Pascal, but one thing we will share in life's end: You also died very young, didn't you?

Pascal: I was thirty-nine years old, and I suffered much during those final days, too. And you're now forty-six? What were you talking about when you stepped in here?

Wilde: About laws and society censoring one's sexual practices. I get outraged when I think about it! Is this too holy a place to speak of such things?

Pascal: It's the best place in the world to talk about things sacred. But let's take a walk through these streets to a place where you're more comfortable.

Wilde: Well, yes…knowing you're going to be brought in here in a box the next time around is not exactly comforting. Where would you like to go?

Pascal: I have an idea, because you might just come to life there...

Wilde: Do I ever miss these cafés! By the way, where'd we lose the Lord Christ? He's not with us.

Pascal: He just stopped to speak to a woman whose child is dying. He's never far from anyone.

Wilde: I see where you're headed. This gallery is a marvelous tribute to what art is meant to be. The great Louvre!

Pascal: This is where we see the image of man overriding the image of God.

Wilde: Oh no! You sound like my wife now! We argued over my being swallowed up by art and beauty. Art was my life. She just couldn't see life in those terms. She railed at me all the time, said I was wasting my life, having lost the absolute. She wrote me a letter once, and I well remember her words.

Pascal: What did she have to say?

Wilde: She and I strongly disagreed on the place of morality in the arts. She held that there was no perfect art without perfect morality, but I insisted that they were two separate things. I celebrate spontaneity. Who really cares whether it aligns with an absolute or not?

But then, I well remember her tender words on one occasion, after a rather intense disagreement on the subject. "Of course," she said, "you have your knowledge to combat my ignorance with! Truly I am no judge that you should appeal to me for opinions, and even if I were, I know that I should judge you rather by your aims than by your work, and you would say I was wrong."

What do you think?

Pascal: The question is more to you now, M. Wilde. She was obviously trying to tell you something while meek in her spirit, but sure in her thoughts.

Wilde: But she also knew that she was ignorant of the subject, except to judge me by my motives. Actually, I think art is more real than life and should hold sway rather than be subject to the dictates of others. That's another thing…people who don't know anything about art passing judgment on it!

Pascal: What do you know about morality? Never mind…

This philosophy on art you're sharing may well be the undoing of any culture. If musicians and artists have no absolutes, they end up caring more about the way the thing is told than about the thing itself, and they slide deeper and deeper till it's their means rather than the ends that matter. And now as we see art beginning to move into the age of machines—

Wilde: I grant that. You know, when I came back from Rome with my new Kodak camera…oh! The pictures were wonderful!

And I began to think of all that pictures could do in art. I wonder what the future is with pictures.

Pascal: That will be the day that distortion masquerades as truth and the imagination will be bloodied. The picture is a seductive thing. It makes unreal what is real and makes real what is unreal. Let's walk through these halls and see what I'm trying to tell you. This is only a foretaste.

Wilde: Look at these grand works of art! Why should the artist not be at complete ease in doing whatever he pleases?

Pascal: If you read the songs of David and Solomon, you'll find out that the first and foremost desire that God seeks in those who come to Him is truth. That is at the core, M. Wilde. That is His desire. Then there's the description of beauty at its best. He called the people to worship the Lord in the *beauty* of *holiness*—these two are inseparable. When beauty is bounded by holiness, the artist soars to the highest. The further one gets from holiness, the greater the potential of violating beauty. Nothing profane can ever be beautiful. The artist who celebrates profanity dabbles in the hideous and the hurtful. You see, M. Wilde, before anything is offered to man, it must first be offered to God. That which God cannot receive because of its vileness must never be offered to a human being for his corruption.

Wilde: Beauty and holiness—not exactly topics that stir the average person, are they, M. Pascal?

Pascal: No. That's because holiness maintains the distance between God and humanity. The artist who refuses to keep that distance goes, in effect, against the very essence of God.

Wilde: But this is where I take offense. Is art really in the realm of the imagination? (How I hate that word, *imagination!*) Maybe there's more pretense in life than in art. The imagination thrives on liberties that the intellect can't always afford. Why are you so afraid to give an artist free rein over his creations?

Pascal: Afraid, did you say? Is that the best word you can find for calling upon the imagination to be submissive to the very Creator of the universe? It may be precisely because the artist who fears nothing or no one makes fearsome expressions as art. Are you really saying that there are no absolutes to limit the imagination? Are you really saying that it has no effect on the viewer or the listener? Your dislike of the word *imagination* notwithstanding, is there no difference between art and profanity?

Wilde: I cannot honestly deny that there were moments. In fact, are you aware of the story that I wrote, M. Pascal, *The Picture of Dorian Gray?*

Pascal: When you ask someone who lived two hundred years before you, who is now living in the eternal, if he knows what you wrote, you're asking to lift the curtain of time in a way that you will have to wait for.

Wilde: Well, I just thought that perhaps…since it's partially lifted already…

Pascal: You always wanted to rush things, didn't you? As a writer, you should know that the greatest author of all has saved the full revelation for the right time.

Wilde: All right, M. Pascal, let me just assume that it will help me to retell the story of Dorian Gray, just because it might do my own soul good.

It's the story of a splendidly attractive young man. An artist made a portrait of him. As the young man admired his own beauty, he wished it would endure permanently and that any riotous and sensual living would leave him untarnished and affect only the picture. Life would be great that way. I still think—

Pascal: No, it wouldn't, and it's because you're not thinking, but wishing…

You pause. Is there a reason?

Wilde: I seem to go in and out of reality, and I'm not sure whether I'm telling you this story or just imagining that I am.

Pascal: Please continue, M. Wilde; I am listening.

Wilde: Dorian got his wish. His life of sensual abandon and lawless living left him completely unaltered in his appearance. But, of course, unknown to him, with every vile act or choice,

Are you really saying that there are no absolutes to limit the imagination? Is there no difference between art and profanity?

BLAISE PASCAL

the portrait he had hidden in the attic registered the consequence on his face. Little by little the countenance was disfigured and marred.

Well, the day came when the artist visited Dorian. You just have to read it, M. Pascal. You're not getting the benefit of the whole story line, just the surface.

Pascal: As every author would say!

Wilde: There's so much in that story!

The artist, of course, was stunned beyond measure when he saw the portrait. He pleaded with Dorian to make amends: "Doesn't it say somewhere, 'Though your sins be as scarlet, they shall be as white as wool'?"

Pascal: Are you asking me, M. Wilde?

Wilde: No, no, that's what the artist said to Dorian. Instead, Dorian reached for a knife and stabbed the artist to death! Something terrible happened then. I saw blood dripping down the front of the picture! I grabbed—

Jesus: You grabbed?

Wilde: You don't miss a thing, do You? I thought You weren't here.

Jesus: Hasn't that been the problem all your life, Oscar? Please continue telling your story.

Wilde: Dorian grabbed the knife and stabbed the picture. With a bloodcurdling scream, he fell to the floor, lifeless.

Well, the story goes that the picture returned to its pristine beauty, and Dorian lay marred and scarred, bearing the marks of his debauched lifestyle.

Jesus: It was a powerful story, relived every day in someone's mind. True to life. Why did you write it?

Wilde: That's art.

Jesus: If that's all it was, why were you hurt when somebody recently saw you coming out of a theater and muttered, "There goes Dorian"?

Wilde: Because…because I'd done to myself what the story merely contained as art. And they should've kept them separate!

Jesus: Did it ever occur to you that for you, the two are no longer separate? Do you know why truth is stranger than fiction?

Wilde: Because we've made fiction to suit ourselves.

Jesus: You couldn't bring yourself to see that the rules you refused to allow to govern your life broke your life. When art and beauty are not governed by rules, they, in turn, break down.

Wilde: Yes, I didn't stop playing. I always was a gambler. I played against the odds. But you see, even in writing that book, the moral side of it was part of my intention, but secondary to the dramatic side. I wanted people to see the beauty of the story, not the moral side of it.

Jesus: You lived as if your life were the dream and your creations were real. When you "awakened," you found the opposite to be true. My prophet Isaiah tells of a man who was hungry. He dreamed one night that he was feasting at a banquet, only to awaken to the reality that it was all a dream. He was still hungry. He tells of a thirsty man who went to sleep one night and dreamed he was drinking from gushing springs of cool water, only to wake up and find he was still thirsty. Such is the illusion under which a generation flirts with beauty and art and thinks they take precedence over truth. They'll awaken one day to find that their dream has left them still empty. You see, this is the danger. First, art imitates life. Then life imitates art. Finally, art becomes the very reason for life, and that's when life breaks down, because life is not fiction…it is plain, hard fact.

Wilde: But what about—

Jesus: It's important that I finish this thought for you, Oscar.

Whether in Rome, Athens, or here in Paris, there are no exceptions. Artists are creative people. It is not so much that artistic expression is fiction. It is more that it impinges upon the senses as a reality till the lines become blurred between fact and fiction, picture and passion, truth and action, thinking and living. A picture takes on a life of its own and sometimes supplants life. Humanity ends up worshiping its own idols and then resembling them.

You said you didn't like the word *imagination.* The images in flights of fancy often become the reality one imagines.

Pascal: I suppose this is where genius gets in the way, by thinking beyond God's vision, M. Wilde. It nearly happened to me as an empiricist; how much more in the arts! If artists do not reflect the purpose of the Creator Himself, they take the place of God and shape reality according to their own image and imagination. In fact, you remember the Sistine Chapel, do you not?

Wilde: That's what I was going to ask you. Are you going to censor Michelangelo now?

Pascal: No, but it was an issue for him as well. Nakedness reduced to art desacralizes the purpose for which the body was made. Nakedness can never be separated from sensuality by the pleasure-driven human heart. And the day it is tried, it reveals not the innocence of the heart, but its corruption.

Morality can never be subservient to beauty. It's the other way around. We see it in the Scriptures. Whenever God's ceremonial law comes into conflict with the moral law, the moral law always wins out. Michelangelo struggled with the unclothed body but justified it by saying he wanted to see man as God sees man.

Wilde: Well?

Pascal: He was not God, M. Wilde. His teacher reminded him of that. Let me say it with all the passion I can muster: It is in vain that men seek within themselves the cure for all their miseries. All their insight leads us only to the knowledge that it is not in ourselves that we discover the true and the good. The philosophers promised them to us, but they were not able to keep their promise. Our principal maladies are pride, which cuts us off from God, and sensuality, which binds us to the earth. If the philosophers have given God to us as an object, it is to make us think we are like Him and resemble Him in our nature. This is the first abyss, to think that we are God. Those who have grasped the vanity of such pretensions have cast us down into the other abyss by leading us to seek our good in lust alone, which is the lot of animals, and makes us no different than animals.

Wilde: I remember reading that in your *Pensées,* M. Pascal. There we have it in a nutshell—your theological statement.

Pascal: Everyone has a theological statement that informs all other decisions. You've had yours, M. Wilde. For you, expression is all that has mattered; everything else was a mask. You wanted absolute freedom in creativity but ignored the limitless capacity of the heart to distort purpose. You missed the potential horror of your dream.

Wilde: What do you mean?

Pascal: As a scientist, I knew that with each new invention would come a new and more dangerous test for the soul. I did think of that when I brought the calculator into being. Someone will take that machine and apply it to more sophisticated inventions.

Jesus: The same is true of pictures. Professing themselves to be wise, men and women will descend into the depths till humanity will be alone with distorted images. The soul will be shaped by this indescribable power, and who will tame the will then? Actually, you saw this very clearly in your struggle, Blaise. Do you remember what you said about philosophy and the imagination—that you can take the world's greatest philosopher and place him on a plank that's wider than necessary, and if there's a precipice below, although his reason may convince him that he's safe, his imagination will prevail?

Pascal: I had no doubt about that illustration.

Wilde: The very thought turns me pale and makes me break into a sweat!

Jesus: That's the strength of the imagination; it overpowers reason. There is more…and that was another issue you wrestled with. You see, in every scene that an artist portrays, there's an unseen but real source doing the portraying and the viewing.

Wilde: What is that?

Jesus: It's the soul. There's either a disfigurement or a wholeness within that shapes the picture and the viewer.

Wilde: I certainly wrestled with that. But here, too, society does not have a right to shape my soul. It's not anybody's business what I do with my body. I act on impulse. That's what set me apart as a crusader of sorts for our rights.

Jesus: Then why were you living in prison with such deep regret? Over what you had done to others?

Wilde: Worse. Over what I had done to myself.

Jesus: I longed to reach you through those years you spent walking backwards toward the altar with your eye on the exit. But let Me ask you, what do you think laws are meant for?

Wilde: To keep us from hurting each other in uncivil ways.

Jesus: And so laws must be at the wish and whim of every new authority?

Wilde: No authority can ever inhibit my sensuality. Nor should it!

Jesus: By your own admission, what you had done to yourself was hurtful. If what you had done to yourself was hurtful, did you think that no one needed to protect others from your disfigurement of them? But go back to your own anguish at that time. You came very close, before your trial was over, to a complete collapse, didn't you? You were on the verge of a complete breakdown. Why was that?

Wilde: Several of the young blackmailing boys and their furious fathers were after me, wanting to press charges. I…yes, that's the other side. They wanted to drag me through hell. I still ache from it all.

Jesus: Do you remember the time you privately asked one of your partners in crime this question: "Did you ever love one of those boys for his own sake?"

Pascal: What a terrifying question!

Jesus: Do you remember that, Oscar?

Wilde: Oh, dear me! Dear me! All private deeds will one day be shouted from the rooftop, won't they?

Jesus: I won't bring their names and faces before you now. But do you remember that?

Wilde: I do, Lord Christ. My enticement came with gentle face but fangs of jagged steel!

Jesus: Don't forget that you were both the enticer and the enticed, and you have evaded the question. What was the answer that you both agreed on?

Wilde: That we had not.

Jesus: Had not what?

Wilde: Had not loved any of them for their own sakes. This is too painful to talk about anymore. These are the fangs that continue to draw my blood.

Jesus: Love for the sake of another is at the core of what is right and wrong. That's at the heart of good laws. Love can never violate the sacred nature of another life.

When I was walking to the cross for you, Oscar, and for the sins of the whole world, some women were crying as I was being led away by My accusers. I looked at those women on the side of the road and said something to them that they didn't understand.

Pascal: You mean when You said, "Do not weep for me; weep for yourselves and for your children"?

Jesus: Yes, because I could see what men and women were doing to themselves and what they were going to do to the very ones they loved. They despised being interfered with and wanted laws to be kept out of their desires to hate and kill. Laws do have a role, Oscar. They have a role to keep men and women from hurting not just the ones they hate, but even the ones they love. It's little wonder you didn't understand laws, because you didn't understand love.

Wilde: How can I deny that? In fact, the love that I thought controlled many of my relationships actually turned into a burning hate.

Jesus: Wanting someone without a commitment to that someone is always one step away from hate; you exhaust the sensual and then want your potential accuser to just be gone from your life. My laws were designed out of love for each and every person so that none would be abused.

Pascal: The Reformers called it the first use of the law, to keep society in check because of God's love for each and every one. The second use is to convict us of sin and reveal our need for God's grace, and the third is to sanctify the person who follows God's laws.

Jesus: Your demand that the law be kept out of your private life is echoed in the streets of lust, Oscar. Is that what you want? Even if the laws allowed you to chase your passions to the limit, there's one thing you'll never change. You cannot escape destruction from within. That's the law I've built into the path of evil so that you'll see the devastation of evil and stop. That law I have built into the very soul of humanity. You yourself said so in *The Picture of Dorian Gray*—the corruption had come from within. Your own words speak of such destruction. You despise the law for telling you what is wrong. Dorian killed the artist for exposing his soul when the artist actually cared for him.

You love your sons, Oscar. You weep over what has happened between you and your family. But you love them. Would you want someone to do to them what you did with the sons and daughters of other fathers? Do you want Me not to care? I have wept over cities and over every man, woman, and child. Again and again I have left ninety-nine in the careful protection of the fold to go looking for the one in danger.

Wilde: I didn't intend to get this far in this side note.

Jesus: Do you really think this is a side note?

Wilde: By discussing the young ones that I hurt?

Jesus: If you question the law, there's a connection, isn't there? But I understand. Most people don't intend to go as far as they do in the seductions of life either. And you are sadly right, Oscar. Someday those who despise laws will triumph, and then they will weep for what they've done to their own children. Have you heard of the Valley of Hinnom in Jerusalem?

Wilde: It got its name from *Gehenna,* didn't it? Meaning "hell"?

Jesus: Yes, because that's where some of the kings offered their children as sacrifices in the brazen arms of an idol. The horror of the children screaming as the flames swallowed them up reminded the people of hell. That's how it got its name. Do you not want Me to care?

The truth is that whenever a fence is removed, it's wise to ask why it was put there in the first place. You can take note of that. When the fence that I first set up around sexuality is removed, it is the beginning of a downward spiral. First, a person will victimize himself, then he will victimize others, and then his very own children—until what was meant to be enjoyed in the sacredness of marriage, in an act of maturity, is reduced to purely the sensual. Ultimately, children will be sacrificed at the altar of a wicked and perverse will. That's when the last stake of the fence will have been removed.

But I have warned the nations of what happens when people are lovers of themselves. I am the giver of freedoms, but I'm also the exactor of consequences.

Wilde: You mean one way or the other we'll pay?

Jesus: One way or the other you'll find out that wickedness breaks, and breaks first within—with relentless effect. Whatever you sow to the flesh, you'll of the flesh reap corruption. Don't be deceived just because you can get some laws changed.

Wilde: So You agree with the pain society inflicted upon me?

Jesus: I thought you said it was nothing compared to what you inflicted upon yourself?

Wilde: I hear You, Lord Christ. I hear You. But something within me keeps screaming out the words with frustration—don't I have the right to victimize myself?

Jesus: And be left to your own devices by a loving God? Besides, no one lives purely with the ramifications only for oneself. Get rid of that illusion! Don't you remember the story of My people on their journey from Egypt to Canaan? How the sin of one destroyed many? The sins of the fathers visit generations to come.

A society that hates laws

that guard the soul

despises not so much the

laws as much as it despises the

very thought of a soul.

JESUS

Wilde: That's one of the most difficult things about my life…so debauched…now watching its imposition upon my family.

Jesus: A society that hates laws that guard the soul despises not so much the laws as much as it despises the very thought of a soul. Those who belong to such a society consider the flesh the totality of their being.

Wilde: I know why You care. You of all beings have my highest admiration. I don't have a problem with You, Lord Christ. There is such compassion in Your voice, such pleading in Your call. Your mercy shines through the Gospels.

Jesus: You cannot separate Me from the law. The law was like a schoolmaster leading to me. I am the fulfillment of the law. I embody the law. The world crucified Me, but it couldn't destroy Me. In bearing that pain, I showed you what the breaking of the law brings. The only difference between the justice system and My crucifixion is that in the justice system *you* pay— hunger, disease, insomnia. In My death, *I* paid—sorrow, isolation, inordinate suffering—to deliver you from the price the law could have exacted.

Wilde: Ironic, isn't it, that it was in prison, where I learned to hate the law, that I saw what so many had done to themselves, becoming coarse, hard, and hate-filled.

You know, I once told a story about a man who caught a

momentary glimpse of this being that hid its face from him. It haunted him with determined frequency, but somehow, no matter how hard he tried, he could never see its face. Finally one day, seduced by pleasure once again, the man entered a long room where the tables were spread and the revelry was to begin.

Suddenly, as if a ghost had brushed past him, he saw the face in a mirror. It was there like a flash and then gone. I begged the face to stay. "Please, please, let me see you," I said, and it came and I saw it. I saw it! I'm sorry I ever did. It's unbearable to even think of it now!

Jesus: I understand.

Wilde: Well, the face stared at me and said, "Look at me. You pursued me from your youth. You will want to see this face no more. This is the face of your soul. And it is horrible."

Jesus: Similar to Dorian Gray. You can't deny that I gave you insights into the seeds of your lifestyle and how they would blossom into the life of your future.

Wilde: I was better at art than at living.

Jesus: You used art as an excuse for your living. You see, it's not the law that's the problem, Oscar. The point you've made is that what you had done to yourself was a lifelong marring of the young, beautiful giftedness that I had given you. But what many others may have missed is that when you were in the

When you were in the throes

of pleasure for pleasure's sake,

you often saw most clearly the

devastation of your soul.

JESUS

throes of pleasure for pleasure's sake, you often saw most clearly the devastation of your soul. Is that not a clue to you of life's purpose, that it can't be found in sensuality? You made a prison for yourself by fleeing from the place that I had given the law in your life.

Wilde: What I pursued devoured me when I caught up with it.

Jesus: These are almost the same words Solomon wrote after he had chased everything under the sun:

"I thought in my heart, 'Come now, I will test you with pleasure to find out what is good.' I wanted to see what was worthwhile for men to do under the sun... I undertook great projects: I built many houses, planted numerous vineyards. I made gardens and parks and planted fruit trees. I owned more flocks than anyone before me. I amassed silver and gold for myself, and the treasure of kings and provinces. I acquired a harem...the delight of the heart of man. I denied myself nothing my eyes desired; I refused my heart no pleasure.

"Yet when I surveyed all that my hands had done and what I had toiled to achieve, everything was meaningless, a chasing after the wind; nothing was gained under the sun."

These are the words of Solomon the king. The world thought he had it all. But in the end he concluded that love for God is the paramount protection against the pollution of desire. And that love should start when one is young.

Wilde: I remember reading that as well.

Jesus: When you understand how it works "under the sun," you realize why pleasure disappoints. That's the key Solomon gives you…that under the sun, chasing pleasure is chasing after the wind.

Wilde: Why do You keep saying, "under the sun"?

Pascal: Can't you see it, M. Wilde? "Under the sun"—the years God has appointed for you in a closed system when the mind of God is shut out, when you live only with temporal values, when the wheels of thought grind out answers that only our bodies crave. You get it, don't you? And you aren't made to live eternally "under the sun."

Wilde: I do, M. Pascal; I do get it. But that's how we all grind out our days. That's why I've stated to a friend that work never seemed to me a reality, but only a way of getting rid of reality. I think it's another one of those masks we wear…"under the sun." And now as I see my own wretchedness and have perhaps only moments left to live, I have only the leftovers of a squandered life and eternity to live in remorse.

Jesus: What seems so difficult for many to grasp is that pleasure is always momentary. You can time it on every occasion. It has no staying power. That's what happens "under the sun"— apart from God. All pleasure, however good, is locked into the sensation of the moment. Was the pleasure in keeping with the way My Father has framed you? If it's in keeping with His will, the mark it leaves upon your conscience will draw you back again to the pleasure, only this time it is pursued for a greater purpose than immediate gratification.

This is something you must understand. To be enduring, pleasure must always come from a prior moral commitment. If not, it is fleeting and empties very quickly. And in every relationship, there must be a moral commitment. Don't ever forget that.

Wilde: Unfortunately, Lord, it seems that I did.

Jesus: That's the pitiful condition of these we see here tonight as we walk this street of different shades of darkness.

Wilde: I see what You're saying about pleasure so clearly now as this body of mine is falling apart, wracked in pain. But these others don't see what they're shaping for their future. And so I have a nagging question to ask You: Why did You make us thus? Why does this body crave pleasure to such a painful limit? We seduce ourselves by what You made us desire. We play with things You wanted us to treat as sacred. We run from things You wanted us to cling to. We make companions of those You told us never to embrace. We clutch in our hands what You wanted us to throw away. We throw away what You wanted us to hold fast to. We dream of things that make life a nightmare. Why this disorder in the way we are made?

Why did You make us thus?

Why does this body crave

pleasure to such a painful limit?

We seduce ourselves by what

You made us desire.

OSCAR WILDE

Jesus: Every power known to man comes with a double edge: one, the knowledge to use it properly, and the other, the great capacity to abuse it. Take any such power, and you'll find that double edge. When I fashioned humanity in the beginning, their hungers were attuned to goodness. But with the capacity to love and serve came the double edge to reject and renounce. The choice to try to live in the garden without any boundaries has reshaped every hunger within the human heart.

It is pivotal that you understand this. Every appetite that is abused reconstitutes desire, and it is that altered desire that the enemy of your soul appeals to.

Wilde: So my hungers are unnatural?

Jesus: They're natural but falsely directed. They're ungodly because by abusing the way those appetites were to be fulfilled, you prioritized your hungers in accordance with the flesh and debased them in the process. It is tyranny to have by one means what is designed to be accomplished by another. When you have it the wrong way, you pollute the very longing until the wrong way becomes the only way, and the right way becomes a burden.

Wilde: You mean wrong actions manufacture further wrong desires?

Jesus: And demean good ones. Have you ever wondered how the steps to temptation really work?

There are three inclinations Satan appeals to and three steps in every temptation. In understanding this, you'll see the distortion. The evil one appeals to three basic hungers—food, power, and pleasure. He wants all of these met autonomously. He demands the miracle for the wrong reason. He calls upon God for the wrong motive. He offers the world, but it isn't his to give. The hungers are all misdirected.

In falling for that temptation, you exalt power to meet your need rather than surrender in humility to God's will. This is the way the tempter takes away your humanity and supplants it with the illusion of omnipotence. He takes away the soul and leaves you with the body.

Wilde: So You're saying that the devil takes your natural limitation and transposes it into an unnatural inclination. I can see that…I think I can see that.

Jesus: Isn't that the classic ploy of wickedness—to keep a semblance of the natural but to distort it to the unnatural?

The three steps are straightforward. The first step begins with a spark of misplaced desire that in turn is inflamed by enticement and finally consumed by the will. Desire, enticement, and the will. My servant James speaks of that.

The natural inclination was subverted in the first garden, Oscar. That's where we go back to. You see, it has nothing to do with why temptation seems to be so strong or why I have made you this way. All these may sound like powerful questions to start with, but in the end it's the quest for one's own law that stalks a person. Every man and woman and child wants to do what's right on his or her terms. These are the steps to imprisoning the heart. First the desire, then the deception, and finally, the decision.

Pascal: If God gives us the privilege of loving one woman, M. Wilde, we want to love two. If He had given us the privilege of loving ten, we would have wanted eleven. Our hunger is to be a law unto ourselves.

Wilde: Then we cannot win over this one.

Jesus: This is where the real miracle begins, Oscar. You cannot win it on your own. New hungers are planted within when I bring new life within you. Without that new life, you can never be victorious. The most flagrant demonstration of the self against God is shown in the very refusal to admit that the wrong way is never satisfying. At the root of the rejection of My way is not reason; it is the corrupted heart that reasons its way to autonomy. Every desire then degenerates away from My Father's will.

You're at the first step. Beginning with an impoverished spirit is the first step to the enrichment of life. You well know that vortex you found yourself trapped in, the battle of self versus God, especially when your mind was capable of such lofty exploits. You see, if an essential part of finding Me is to realize one's own lowly condition, then the self-intoxicated person has to come a long way down.

Wilde: But it's more than humility for the moment—coming down—isn't it? We can all come down for a moment. It's staying down.

Jesus: Pride is at the root of sin, humility at the root of righteousness. You thought you could reverse that.

Wilde: Yes, you're both staring at one who embodied that perversion. I started with almost everything in life that a young man would want. I let myself be lured into long spells of senseless and sensual ease. I amused myself with being a flaneur, a dandy, a man of fashion. I surrounded myself with smaller natures and meaner minds. I became the spendthrift of my own genius, and to waste an eternal youth gave me a curious joy. Tired of being on the heights, I deliberately went to the depths in search of a new sensation. What paradox was to me in the sphere of thought, perversity became to me in the sphere of passion. Desire at the end was a malady, madness, or both. I grew careless of the lives of others. I took pleasure where it pleased me and passed on. I forgot that every little action of the common day makes or unmakes character and that, therefore, what one has done in the secret chamber, one has someday to cry aloud on the housetop. I ceased to be lord over myself. I was no longer the captain of my soul and did not know it. I allowed pleasure to dominate me. I ended in horrible disgrace. There is only one thing for me now: absolute humility.

Jesus: If you choose what is right, there's still hope, Oscar.

Wilde: What does one ask for when the clock is ticking with such speed? How do I work through this struggle? May I push my question a little further? This body…this wretched body. Talk to me a little more about this body that feels, that wants, that hungers, that seeks the touch.

Jesus: The challenge of the heart is to judge as nothing everything that must in the end return to nothing: the heavens and the earth, one's own spirit and body, one's kinsmen and friends and enemies, wealth and poverty, disgrace, prosperity, good reputation, health, and so on—anything, in short, that endures for a shorter time than the soul does is incapable of satisfying the soul, which earnestly desires to be established in a felicity as durable as itself.

Wilde: Please, keep talking, Lord Christ. I'm framing my final questions.

Jesus: I really must not proceed until you've grasped this.

Wilde: But how can one treat things that are temporary as nothing? Just because they're temporary? I know this body is temporary. But so is this life. Must I treat it as nothing?

Jesus: I said that anything that endures for a shorter time than the soul does is incapable of satisfying the soul.

Wilde: Which means I shouldn't pursue anything that doesn't satisfy the soul? Where does the body fit into all of this..."the flesh," as You often call it?

Jesus: No, it doesn't mean you shouldn't pursue anything that doesn't satisfy the soul. But it does mean that anything that violates the soul destroys it; what is permanent is destroyed by what is temporary.

Wilde: There's a hierarchy of pleasure, then?

Jesus: Of course there is, Oscar. Each gratifying pleasure is like the rung of a ladder. Each is able to carry you only a little further but is not able to sustain you. All of those pleasures are "under the sun."

Wilde: It's true...my pleasure always demanded just one step more.

Jesus: But here's your answer. In seeking pleasure, you pursued the body and lost the person. You sought the sensation and sacrificed the individual. You see, in pursuing the sacred, you exalt the person and the sensation follows. Life then makes sense. In pursuing sensuality, you exalt the body and profane the person. It's like emptying a container and throwing it away. Life, then, becomes just a container. Living becomes senseless.

You wanted sexual promiscuity. It's written into the nature of sexuality that perversion empties pleasure of the meaning for which it was created. The body was not made for that. The binding of a man and woman in the one-flesh union is indicative of the embrace of their spirits. As I've said to you, the primacy of the person must always be kept intact. When that's lost, the sexual act is a stealer of pleasure.

Wilde: What I'm hearing You say is that all this passion You've designed us with finds no room for expression merely in the body. In thinking I was finding a perfect expression for passion, I exhausted passion itself.

Jesus: The perfect expression for passion is in the soul—when you love the Lord your God with all your heart and mind and soul and strength. That communion of your person with the person of God enables you to see every other person as precious in His sight. The body becomes His temple. That takes you beyond the sun—

Pascal: And comes only through His Son. Every other passion will exhaust itself. Pleasures are meant to point you to the greatest pleasure of all, the presence of our heavenly Father.

Wilde: I never knew that—that the closer the pleasure is in keeping with Your will, Lord Christ, the closer I come to You.

Jesus: This is the greatest dignity given to you, Oscar—that I desire that communion with you that I have with My Father.

Wilde: And that's the most beautiful gift.

Jesus: The valley, the mountain, the created order all speak of

The ultimate glimpse of rapture
is to glimpse My Father,
who has made you to see things
and enabled you to see through
them until there is nothing
beyond Him.

JESUS

My glory. But even they will pass away, because the ultimate glimpse of rapture is to glimpse My Father, who has made you to see things and enabled you to see through them until there is nothing beyond Him.

Pascal: It's the glory of personality, M. Wilde, fulfilled in finding the very person of God.

Wilde: Just as we distort the natural desires by reshaping the hunger, we destroy fulfillment by diminishing the person.

Pascal: It's out of the sense of one's own immortality that a sinner must give vent to an elevated sense so transcendent that it does not pause at beauty or even the peak of the heavens nor with the angels nor with any created beings, however admirable. The soul rises to its highest, beyond all creatures, when its swelling heart beats at the very throne of God, where it finds repose at last. Here it confronts that absolute, who incorporates in Himself all that is good and eternal. One who can never cease to be and one who can fill the deepest yearning to the highest degree.

Wilde: My heart bursts with sorrow as I see what I've done! This is where I lost it in my marriage as well. Marriage became an idea, a thing of convenience to me. I lost the person I was married to.

Pascal: You weep over a lost love in your wife and rightly so. Your wife was not just another body. This is where mathematics breaks down. One and one do not make two in relationships. One and one make an infinite consummation in the act of lifelong commitment. Life is not defined by mathematics or scientific formulae. Your wife's name sets her apart in your mind so that when her name is uttered, you should think only of that one who breathes into your soul a distinct aura of love and tenderness.

Wilde: You both are reading me too well.

Jesus: But that's not all you meant, is it, Oscar? The depth of sadness in your voice speaks more than the words.

Wilde: You truly are a reader of the heart, Lord Christ. Yes, I was thinking about when I went to see her grave in Genoa a year after she died. Her tombstone just said "Constance Mary." And below that, the words "He shall wipe away every tear."

Jesus: I know your sadness isn't just remorse that you were the cause of her tears.

Wilde: No, I feel agony because she left out her last name— just "Constance Mary." That hurts. Nobody would know she was my wife. I was lost to her. She must've felt completely alone. She died without my name as hers.

I really loved Constance, yet I walked away from her. I mean…I mean, even after my time in prison, I had determined that I would right my ways and go back to her…that our love would blossom again. We were writing, You know. We were setting the date to reunite. Oh, that wretched desire that ruined me! I trampled her forgiving heart under my selfish pleasure once again!

Jesus: I know how deeply you fought that battle of the soul. Yet you returned to what you had turned from in such deep remorse in prison. Again and again I tried to reach you before you returned to the destruction that had brought you down in the first place. But you would not listen.

Wilde: I just caved in when I got too close to the temptation again. This horrid relationship from the past—my friendship and romance with him, which I vowed I'd never pick up again—came right back. I was once more in the very hell I had run from. I was holding on to the very thing You told me to flee. I threw away the very thing You wanted me to cling to.

I lost it all, Lord Christ! When I heard that I wouldn't even see my children… How does this all happen? I'm heartsick over it all.

Jesus: You put your finger on the pulse of it all. Your reason wasn't enough to keep you from going back to your sordid life.

Pascal: That's why I've said that the heart has its reasons that reason does not know. The heart is desperately wicked, and until that heart is turned over to the Lord Christ, you'll never win it by reason.

Wilde: No amount of inner argument that I was headed in the wrong direction saved the day for me.

Jesus: This is why I've said that the philosopher can't take you to God. There's a limitation to reason. The heart flees even when reason counters it, because it doesn't wish to belong to anything that results in a surrender of self.

But listen carefully, Oscar, because the hour strikes. Just as in sensual pleasure you never found satisfaction, now in utter surprise, in the depths of sorrow you may find the crux of the answer.

Wilde: Wait just a moment. Did You purposely use the word *crux?*

Jesus: All these years of preparing you may well be showing through now, Oscar. Yes, there is a crux. There is a "cross" of the matter. There's something in brokenness that the well person seldom sees.

Wilde: It was in the lap of sorrow, when the cup of pleasure had been emptied, that I stared at Your cross.

Jesus: In that strange hell called prison, you longed for the power of freedom within. Pleasure took you astray, and pain brought you back. It happens all too often.

Wilde: Is pleasure the trap that, when sprung, brings pain to the soul? And is pain often the process through which true pleasure finally looms clear? It was what I refused to admit about pleasure that cost me everything.

I made an unexpected discovery in prison: Where there is sorrow, there is holy ground. Someday people will realize what that means. They'll know nothing of life till they do. Prosperity, pleasure, and success may be rough of grain and common in fiber, but sorrow is the most sensitive of created things.

Jesus: There was a second garden, Oscar. I was not deceived by the tempter because My singular desire was to do the will of My Father. I couldn't be enticed to do the wrong thing because My desire was to please My Father. And that was what the temptation that came to a climax in the second garden was all about.

Wilde: Are You speaking about Gethsemane?

Jesus: Yes. As a linguist, you know that the name means "an oil press." Gethsemane was full of olive trees, and there was an oil press there. And just as the olive is compressed till it yields its oil, I was pressed to shed My blood for you. My heart was weighed down. In My desire to do the will of My Father, I was willing to be crushed for you, Oscar. This was the very reason I had come. The temptation that was placed before Me was to bypass the cross.

But I offer you a more excellent way than the way of the world. Arguers look for reasons and stumble at the cross. Power-seekers look for force and are embarrassed by the cross. But those who understand the heart of God see the wisdom of

His way to change the heart. The world doesn't see it, and that's why the enticements of these bright, glistening cities seem like life to you when they are really the way of death. My cross may seem like the way of death, but it really is the one true way to life. The excruciating pain of the cross was the price that had to be paid.

Wilde: Your use of *crux* took me off guard. Doesn't *excruciating* come from Latin and mean "out of the cross"?

Jesus: The cross is the ultimate expression of sorrow and pain combined. It's because the price was paid at the cross that the law is affirmed and transcended. It was at that place that your ultimate worth was upheld. It's because My heart was broken that I'm able to heal yours. Blaise was right—all truths are governed by laws. This one is the way of life and death. I reach out to you through the price I paid for you. I am the artist that humanity sacrificed because I pointed out the defacement of sin.

Wilde: And You knew that when You came to make that revelation, You'd be killed.

Jesus: That's how the law of love works, Oscar. I was willing to lay down My life for those I love. Those who deny Me, I will also deny. Love cannot be coerced. But this is where grace triumphs where laws fail. And in that sense you're right—laws are a weaker form of eliciting compliance. I came as a fulfillment of the law, but at the same time I transcend it.

You said something once that I want you to say again, because it encapsulates both law and grace. Do you remember the statement you made about love touching a wound?

Wilde: I said that a wound bleeds when any hand but the hand of love touches it, and even then it must bleed again, though not in pain.

Jesus: That's the best expression you made of how law works and how grace transcends it without violating it. Once love has touched your wounds, your eyes see suffering in a different light. The ultimate transaction takes place when you see this world through My sufferings and death for you. You remember what I said to you earlier, that the pain and brokenness of your sin can lead you to see the reality of eternity when you view it through the pain that I suffered apart from any sin of My own?

Wilde: It's all coming together. Through the Cross, the real miracle is offered—that of a changed life and heart. Is that right?

Jesus: Yes. Pleasure and pain are not the objects themselves. You felt the pain in prison, but it wasn't enough to keep you from going right back to what took you there in the first place. Pain and pleasure are pointers to what ultimately matters. Only one who lives a crucified life understands these emotions in the way they were intended to be understood.

That's why My apostle Paul said he desired to know nothing among humanity "except Jesus Christ and Him crucified." That's the defining window of life. That's what the world refuses to see. It's only when you see life through My death for you that you see the pain in illicit pleasure. He who does not understand the Cross does not understand My gospel—it will be foolishness to some and a stumbling block to others. He who misses the Cross will always misread pleasure.

Pascal: That, may I say, was what I did not learn at what I've often called my first conversion. It was only eight years later that every passion burned for God and none else. This transformation can be accomplished only through the work of God's Holy Spirit, M. Wilde. When that happens, a new fire burns in the soul. That's why I call the night of my conversion the "night of fire"—I had new passions, new hungers.

Wilde: Is that why you mentioned Mary Magdalene and Moses in this little record of what happened that "night of fire," M. Pascal?

Pascal: Indeed, for a time neither Mary nor Moses recognized that they were in the presence of God. You remember that Mary mistook Him to be the gardener?

Wilde: As I did. I suppose my problem is that one or two encounters were not enough for me. It takes submission to His grace and His power.

He who does not understand the Cross does not understand My gospel—it will be foolishness to some and a stumbling block to others. He who misses the Cross will always misread pleasure.

JESUS

I fled Him, down the nights and down the days;
    I fled Him, down the arches of the years;
I fled Him, down the labyrinthine ways
    Of my own mind; and in the mist of tears
I hid from Him…

Pascal: Francis Thompson?

Wilde: Yes, I read him often.

Jesus: You've run from Me for too long, Oscar. This is your final hour. You stand between life and death. I must leave you now, and your mind must face its choice.

Wilde: And my face will reveal my mind. Wait…wait, Lord Christ, not yet, please. Can't we step into this café one last time? Café Les Deux Magots. Yes, the hours I spent here. Maybe it was symbolic. You see, right from here I could look across at Saint-Germain-des-Prés. But the way I look now, I doubt the waiter would even recognize me. See, he even asked me what I wanted. Never used to…always knew. I must look pitiful.

Jesus: Some bread and fish for Me, you think? To prove all this is real?

Wilde: No, I just don't want this time to end.

Jesus: Before I go, Oscar, I want you to see this picture.

Wilde: Where did You get that? It's hard to believe I looked like that once upon a time, pure and unspoiled during my days at school. Why are You showing this to me?

Jesus: Be careful what you do with it.

Wilde: I can't believe that a countenance as lovely as that now looks like this. Waiter, please bring me a knife…a sharp one!

Pascal: Why do you want that?

Jesus: Just watch the battle between truth and fiction, and you will see that you were right.

Wilde: You know what's coming, don't You, Lord Christ?

Jesus: Better than you do.

Wilde: Aren't You going to stop me?

Jesus: I want you to see your own heart…and Mine.

Wilde: I'm going to do this with my eyes shut and get my feelings uncorked, once and for all. It seems a fitting end.

Pascal: Why are you raising the knife in the air like that, M. Wilde? Wait!

Wilde: What was that scream I heard? It's done…it's done. I've stabbed the innocence and destroyed my past! Dare I look at the picture?

Jesus: Yes, and you will see My face no more until—

Wilde: Lord Christ! This doesn't look like me; You've switched the picture on me! This isn't my face…it's Yours! There's no beauty in it. I mean…I've stabbed You. You took this deadly blow from me…for me? You switched the pictures, didn't You?

Don't leave me now. Please, where did You go…where have they gone? Don't leave. Where are they?

Ross: What are you talking about, Oscar? I told you not to leave when you said there was a vision coming over you. There's no one else here.

Wilde: Robbie! Robbie, I just talked to Christ at the cemetery…at Père Lachaise!

Ross: There's no Christ there, Oscar. There's only the gardener who tends the graves. You're hallucinating.

Wilde: No, I'm not. Robbie, that wasn't a gardener. Please…do me a favor. Read me those stanzas about Christ I wrote in *The Ballad of Reading Gaol*. The lines I penned after I left prison. It's on my table by the bed here. Please, read those words to me.

Ross: But it's so long, Oscar.

Wilde: Just some of the stanzas, please…about the law…about Christ.

Ross:

> I never saw sad men who looked
> > With such a wistful eye
> Upon that little tent of blue
> > We prisoners called the sky,
> And at every careless cloud that passed
> > In happy freedom by.

For Man's grim Justice goes its way,
    And will not swerve aside:
It slays the weak, it slays the strong,
    It has a deadly stride:
With iron heel it slays the strong,
    The monstrous parricide!

And as one sees most fearful things
    In the crystal of a dream,
We saw the greasy hempen rope
    Hooked to the blackened beam,
And heard the prayer the hangman's snare
    Strangled into a scream.

And all the woe that moved him so
    That he gave that bitter cry,
And the wild regrets, and the bloody sweats,
    None knew so well as I:
For he who lives more lives than one
    More deaths than one must die.

I know not whether Laws be right,
    Or whether Laws be wrong;
All that we know who lie in gaol
    Is that the wall is strong;
And that each day is like a year,
    A year whose days are long.

But this I know, that every Law
    That men have made for Man,
Since first Man took his brother's life,
    And the sad world began,
But straws the wheat and saves the chaff
    With a most evil fan.

And thus we rust Life's iron chain
    Degraded and alone:
And some men curse, and some men weep,
    And some men make no moan:
But God's eternal Laws are kind
    And break the heart of stone.

And every human heart that breaks,
    In prison-cell or yard,
Is as that broken box that gave
    Its treasure to the Lord,
And filled the unclean leper's house
    With the scent of costliest nard.

Ah! happy they whose hearts can break
    And peace of pardon win!
How else may man make straight his plan
    And cleanse his soul from Sin?
How else but through a broken heart
    May Lord Christ enter in?

And he of the swollen purple throat,
    And the stark and staring eyes,
Waits for the holy hands that took
    The Thief to Paradise;
And a broken and a contrite heart
    The Lord will not despise.

The man in red who reads the Law
    Gave him three weeks of life,
Three little weeks in which to heal
    His soul of his soul's strife,
And cleanse from every blot of blood
    The hand that held the knife.

And with tears of blood he cleansed the hand,
    The hand that held the steel:
For only blood can wipe out blood,
    And only tears can heal:
And the crimson stain that was of Cain
    Became Christ's snow-white seal.

Wilde:

And there, till Christ call forth the dead,
    In silence let me lie:
No need to waste the foolish tear,
    Or heave the windy sigh:
For I have killed the thing I loved
    And so I have to die.

Only the Blood of Christ can cleanse
    A sinner such as I.

Ross: It's very powerful. I can barely contain my own guilt as I read it.

Wilde: Call a priest, please. Do it right now.

Ross: I'm not sure what all this means, but I'll honor your plea. Good-bye, friend.

Wilde: I've never been sure of anything all my life, Robbie. I want to be sure of at least one thing. Please, call him. Now, please...now.

Ross: Your face is changing, Oscar. And the change seems to be coming from the inside. Oscar, is this happening...or is this my imagination?

EPILOGUE

On November 29, 1900, Father Cuthbert Dunne came to Oscar Wilde's bedside and in his words, "Mr. Wilde received the Sacrament of Extreme Unction." The next day at two o'clock in the afternoon, Wilde sat up in bed, gasped, sighed, and sank back onto the pillow. There were no last words. One friend stated with irony, "It was not a religion with which he could live, but one he clearly wanted to die in…. His decision was the best one he ever made."

On December 3, the funeral was held at Saint-Germain-des-Prés and the bills paid for by a friend. There was no music and no choir. Father Dunne said the mass. Black horses pulled an undecorated hearse, marked with the number thirteen, followed by about fifty well-wishers and friends. He was first buried in a suburban cemetery in Bagneux. In 1909, his remains were moved to Père Lachaise.

On one side of his monument is the verse from *The Ballad of Reading Gaol* cited in the prologue. On the other side are the words from Job 29:22—"After I had spoken, they spoke no more; my words fell gently on their ears."

Apart from any theological questions about his last hours and the rites administered, there is little doubt that in a most profound sense, Wilde's was a life tossed between the sensual and the spiritual—indeed, a life terribly misspent. To debate whether he was genuinely repentant or not is both to grasp the point and to miss it. We grasp it in the sense that there is a tragic side to a deathbed conversion, if indeed there was one. There are mixed feelings about those last moments and about what one has called a "late convert's hell." Yes, much is forgiven, but how much was lost, and how many were plundered by such reckless living before the awakening moment. One can only weep for the loss of all the years that could have been spent in the investment of a brilliant mind for the cause of the Lord.

But it is to miss the point because we can only leave the unknown in the hands of God, who has assured us in His Word that the judge of all the earth will do right. There are those who receive a reward from the "landlord's" gracious hand even though they came to work in His vineyard at the eleventh hour. And so we must leave Wilde's destiny in the hands of our heavenly Father. I cannot help but think of the following words penned by Isaac Watts. If Wilde's repentance was genuine, these words could well have been written by him:

Alas! and did my Savior bleed
  And did my Sovereign die?
Would He devote that sacred head
  For such a worm as I?

Was it for crimes that I had done
  He groaned upon the tree?
Amazing pity! grace unknown!
  And love beyond degree!

A study of Wilde's life reveals with no mistake that the gift of sexuality is a precious gift from God; any perversion of it in any form plunders the sacred and denudes beauty. Anything that is beautiful is governed by laws. The laws are there for its protection because it does not take much to destroy beauty. A work of art that takes years to create can be desecrated in seconds.

In a society that has gone pleasure-mad, we would do well to go back to the author of life and see what His plan is. If we do not, we destroy the beautiful and live with the hideous, all the while masking it by our pretense that all is well. Those who honor what He intended for us to honor will find fulfillment. Those who desecrate what He has made sacred will leave themselves empty and ravaged. At a time in our cultural struggle when sex and sexuality create huge divisions among us, we would do well to remember that the enjoyment of sex was not man's idea, but God's. But to enjoy it by ungodly means is man's idea, not God's.

May you find Oscar Wilde's story a telling lesson on what a tragedy life becomes when it loses its way in the name of pleasure, at the cost of the sacred. God desires that we live a life of fulfillment and has reminded us that we will find eternal pleasure only in knowing Him and loving Him with all of our hearts. May the fire of His joy and presence be your trust, your experience, and your delight.

Multnomah Publishers

The publisher and author would love to hear your comments about this book. *Please contact us at:* www.multnomah.net/conversations

Bibliography

Oscar Wilde

Belford, Barbara. *Oscar Wilde: A Certain Genius.* New York: Random House, 2000.

Wilde, Oscar. *Collected Works of Oscar Wilde.* Hertfordshire, England: Wordsworth Editions, 1997.

Ellmann, Richard. *Oscar Wilde.* New York: Vintage Books, 1988.

Holland, Vyvyan. *Son of Oscar Wilde.* Rev. ed. New York: Carroll & Graf Publishers, 1999.

Pearce, Joseph. *The Unmasking of Oscar Wilde.* London: HarperCollins Publishers, 2000.

Blaise Pascal

Morris, Thomas V. *Making Sense of It All: Pascal and the Meaning of Life.* Grand Rapids, Mich.: William B. Eerdmans Publishing Company, 1992.

O'Connell, Marvin R. *Blaise Pascal: Reasons of the Heart.* Grand Rapids, Mich.: William B. Eerdmans Publishing Company, 1997.

Other

Dostoevsky, Fyodor. "The Grand Inquisitor." In *The Brothers Karamazov.* Translated by Constance Garnett. Garden City, N.Y.: The International Collectors Library, n.d.

Why Do They Call It Good When We Call It Evil?

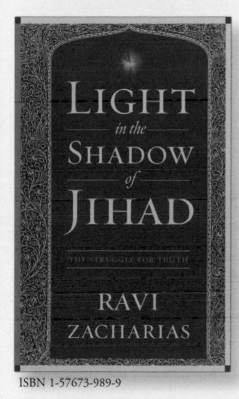

ISBN 1-57673-989-9

The terrorists who brought death to thousands said they did it in God's name. Thousands of Christians around the world gathered in churches to pray for peace, while others blamed the very idea of God for the tragedy. Ravi Zacharias deals with five of the major questions on people's minds after September 11:

- *Is this true Islam or a fanatical counterfeit?*

- *In what ways does the relationship between church and state change a nation's view of religion and affect its culture?*

- *Is religion dangerous to a culture?*

- *Was there a prophecy that this would happen?*

- *Where does this leave the future?*

"If we find those answers," writes Zacharias, "they will spell life, steadying the soul even though the heart still aches."

STEP INTO A LONG-TAIL BOAT ON THE RIVER OF KINGS

…and become immersed in an imaginary conversation between Jesus Christ and Gautama Buddha.

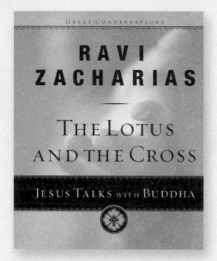

"This captivating dialogue not only clears up confusion about the claims of Christ and Buddha, it provides us with a highly entertaining read."

—CHUCK COLSON

"…this unique drama will educate, enthrall, and enlighten you—and everyone you share it with for years to come."

—BRUCE WILKINSON, author of the *NY Times* #1 bestseller *The Prayer of Jabez*

- Both talked about the "self," but one denied it even existed.
- Both felt the pain of human suffering, but each had a radically different response to it.
- Both addressed our deepest hungers, but one saw them as an impediment, the other as a clue.
- Both have earned a worldwide following—but their answers are worlds apart.

Jesus and Buddha agreed that Truth could withstand scrutiny. Listen in as the Soul of Truth speaks with the Heart of Compassion. It could change your life.

ISBN 1-57673-854-X